Self - Determination under International Law - A Timely Consideration?

By

Haywood Roberts, Esq.

All rights reserved, Copyright 2021

Introduction:

As an author I take no position on the issues covered in this short book. It is intended not as an in-depth study of the issue but more of an introduction to the issue and the complexities involved. It does seem a time to give the matter serious scholarly consideration.

There is little question that in the months and years ahead we will see attempts to use self-determination to create new nation states and so the issue deserves the most careful and measured attention. The ramifications are significant and while animal spirits may be aroused it is hoped these can be tempered by reason and careful thought.

As with other nations since WWII the discord that exists within the current nation states is resulting in consideration of whether a plebiscite may be in order to consider the rights of the people to self-determination. A plebiscite argued by some can address whether the people of certain sub national groups desire a separation in order to resolve the civil dispute that is occurring within their borders. Such a plebiscite could be desirable, whatever its outcome, to avert what may become more than oratory. A plebiscite could be a prelude to the formation of a new union within current nation states similar to the new nations created out of the former Yugoslavia or Czechoslovakia. But there are serious barriers to such a separation and therefore any consideration of the issue must take into account both the advantages and disadvantages of separating a sub national group from its prior union. While the issue might seem a simple one carrying out such a separation is far from simple or easy.

Consideration of the right of self-determination and its legal basis was discussed in a 1965 review of the rights of self-determination in the Duke Law Journal authored by M.K. Nawaz with research by Robert Scott, then a research assistant to Arthur Larson, director of the World Rule of Law Center at Duke University and former Director of the USIA. Title of the article is "The meaning and range of the principle of self-determination" and which may be found for download at: https://scholarship.law.duke.edu/dlj/vol14/iss1/6/

Formation of a new union of states being proposed by some within the current United States (Texas and California being two) could consider possible inclusion of the people of various states whose populations have serious disagreement with the bi-coastal political classes as well as those in the bi-coastal states whose views differ from those in the interior of the country. Whether the population of all these states or only some of them would desire a separation from the current union can be only be decided by a monitored plebiscite. And such a plebiscite should occur only after a debate of the serious issues involved.

It is not underestimated the difficulty of such a separation nor the hostility to it, not the least from major corporations, Silicon Valley, billionaire plutocrats and the old-line media empires or the bi-coastal political class currently in control of the government of the United States. But as with the original Declaration of Independence that led to the formation of the current union of states there comes a time when the oppression of a people by political groups in power requires consideration of such a separation. The results of the 2020 election and questions some have about the validity of the results of that election as well as the apparent inability of our institutions to allow for an airing of evidence to prove or disprove the charges of irregularities along with the likely changes in the fundamental character of the government of the current United States raises the issue of whether just such a separation is now to be seriously considered under the concept of self-determination. It is therefore a time to give the concept of self- determination careful examination.

At the present time there is no serious movement toward such separation of states but as we see more and more suppression of viewpoints that do not agree with the bi-coastal ruling class we may begin to see more and more thought given to possible separation of states through self-determination. There have been nascent attempts in Texas and California in this regard, but they have not garnered support enough to give them serious consideration. How long it will take for this to bubble to the surface and become a real possibility is difficult to determine. Most likely it will take a few years yet but that may well depend on how much suppression is imposed on those whose lives differ so widely from the ruling class. So far, we see no attempt at accommodation or reconciliation. Quite the contrary and if totalitarian Orwellian tactics advance it is this which most likely will see this movement toward a new union of states gain momentum. Before then it is time to consider many of the issues involved. Both the history of self-determination and its application both legally and politically as well as economically will be considered along with the case studies of Scotland, Catalonia, and Quebec where the issue has arisen and in Yugoslavia and Czechoslovakia where separation of sub national groups has in fact resulted in new nation states.

Chapter One: The concept of self determination

The concept of self-determination has its roots in history starting in the modern era with the Declaration of Independence in the United States and later in the French Revolution. Repeated perhaps in Lincoln's Gettysburg address "government of the people, by the people and for the people." And today his prophetic words regarding that government rings with enduring truth when he asked in that same speech "if that government can long endure." So, the question becomes at what point does a division of a people rise to the level where those who feel themselves oppressed by the then ruling class have the right to cast themselves off into a newly formed governmental structure?

Following WWI and the formation of the League of Nations the concept of the rights of a people to self- determination gained both academic and legal justification. And this continued after WWII with the breaking up on many colonial empires that remained as one people after another sought self-government and new national status.

Woodrow Wilson whose ideas formed the basis of the League of Nations expressed his concept of self-determination as the right of self-government. He was among, if not the first, to use the term "self-determination" when he spoke that "national aspirations of peoples must be respected; people may now be dominated and governed only by their own consent. 'Self-determination' is not a mere phrase it is an imperative principle of action...." 1 The Public Papers of Woodrow Wilson, War and Peace 180 (Baker & Dodd ed 1927).

More recently Kur Rabl has stated that in historical context the term "self-determination" has come to mean that "...no people must be forced to live under foreign domination or under a constitutional system which it does not agree to." Rabl, Das

Selbstbestimmungsrecht Der Volker 272 (1963).

Encyclopedia Britannica defines Self-Determination as "the process by which a group of people, usually possessing a certain degree of national consciousness, form their own state and choose their own government."
https://www.britannica.com/topic/self-determination

While the League of Nations in the modern era set forth the concept of Self Determination it found far deeper roots in the formation of the United Nations. In Article I(2) of the United Nations Charter it is expressed that one of the purposes of the United Nations is " friendly relations among nations based on respect for the principles of equal rights and the right of self-determination of peoples." And Article 55 expresses the same sentiment.
https://www.un.org/en/charter-united-nations/

In the Dumbarton Oaks conference on the formation of the United Nations it should be noted that one subcommittee expressed the view that while the concepts in Article I were meant to confirm the rights of a people to self- determination it "…implied the right of self-government and not the right of secession." But this subcommittee report is hardly determinative as there was a division of opinion of the drafters. Doc No 343, I,1,16,6 U.N. Conf Org Doc 296 (1945). And the full committee expressed its views somewhat differently in that it expressed that the concept of self-determination "…that an essential element of the expression of the principle in question (e.g., self-determination) is the free and genuine expression of the will of the people…" Doc No 944, I, 1, 34,1 6 U.N. Conf Intl Org Docs 445, 455 (1945)

One author commenting on the United Nations Charter as regards self - determination notes that: "On the positive side this would mean a right to claim territorial changes in accordance with the wishes of the population. On the negative side it would mean that no territory could be ceded unless confirmed by a plebiscite." Ross, Constitution of the United Nations, 135 (1950). And it seems clear as one author stated that "applied without discernment, self-determination would lead to anarchy." DeVisscher, Theory and Reality in International Law 128 (1957)/

Whatever the academic view of self-determination there is no question that in the end it is the will of the people that is determinative in their self-government. This book will now discuss and try to consider how a people might express their will in such a way as to reorder the government under which they are governed. A subject that is likely to engender strong feelings and strong disagreement between those who wish a separation from their existing government and those ruling over them in their existing form of government.

Chapter Two: Modern discussion of rights of self determination

A recent article in the LA Times has discussed a number of recent attempts to start a secession movement in a variety of states principally in California by liberals angry at Trump and by Texans angry at those same liberals. https://www.latimes.com/opinion/story/2020-12-13/column-are-republicans-like-rush-limbaugh-serious-about-a-secession-movement

And that article expresses alarm at a recent broadcast by Rush Limbaugh in which he raised the issue of secession. The article quotes him as follows: " I actually think that we're trending toward secession. I see more and more people asking what in the world do we have in common with the people who live in, say, New York? ... There cannot be a peaceful coexistence of two completely different theories of life, theories of government, theories of how we manage our affairs. We can't be in this dire a conflict without something giving somewhere along the way."

This raises squarely the concept of self-determination and how it can be applied in the modern era within a nation state such as the United States. Since the Civil War (and certainly before) the issue of secession has been raised with even cities and counties attempting to secede from the Union. More serious efforts have been made by those proposing a Republic of California or a Republic of Texas. And in 2009 Texas Governor Rick Perry raised the specter of secession for Texas.

A recent book by Richard Kreitner has discussed the issue of secession in American political life from the ultimate act of secession in the American Revolution. "Break It Up: Secession, Division, and the Secret History of America's Imperfect Union" (2020) Written from a progressive liberal point of view not many conservatives will agree with the view of history or the legal aspects of secession. But it does throw light on the subject, albeit with a viewpoint. But in contentious times competing points of view must be examined. Especially with as serious a subject as the breakup of a nation.

And lest we think this is not a current movement this item from September 2020 shows a continuation of the efforts in California. https://www.sanjoseinside.com/news/california-secede-one-group-got-a-key-approval-last-week-to-try/ And with the changes in the US government after the 2020 elections the movement in California probably for now has less of a change of succeeding or seceding.

On the other hand, the movement in Texas may just accelerate. As this recent article suggests. https://www.businessinsider.com/texit-texas-state-lawmaker-suggests-referendum-to-secede-from-us-2020-12 While there does not yet appear to be momentum regarding this proposal even within the Texas Republican party a lot may depend on what the Biden administration proposes and enacts into law in coming months and years.

When it comes to interpreting and practice under the United Nations Charter commentary continues to support the right of peoples within a state to make a decision to form a new governmental unit if they so choose. For example, the representative for Cyprus to the General Assembly made this point. "It (self-determination) includes all peoples, in whatever land and in whatever circumstances they are dominated and whatever means they are deprived of their inalienable right to self-determination and freedom." U.N. Gen. Assembly Off. Rec. 15th Sess. Plenary, 1256 (A/PV.945) (1960). Similar views have been expressed on numerous occasions before the General Assembly as set for the in the Duke Law Journal article on Self-Determination.

It is clear that the rise of globalism and anti- nationalism is in direct conflict with the concept of self-determination and will come as no surprise that the existing nation states oppose the recognition of sub national groups that express a desire for independence and expression of their self-determination. Add to this the global corporate world and you have powerful forces opposing the separation of sub national groups no matter how strong the feelings in those groups for a new and independent state. In Iraq the Kurds are perhaps a perfect example with both Turkey and Iraq opposed to creation of a Kurdish state. There are economic, ethnic, religious and political counter forces that both encourage and deter the creation of a new state within the boundaries of a current nation state.

In light of the political vitriol that currently swirls within the dialog in the United States perhaps an example from abroad may make for a useful case study. So, we turn next to the efforts of the Scottish people to separate themselves from Great Britain, the Catalonians wish to separate from Spain and the people of the province of Quebec in Canda. While the first referendum on this resulted in a vote to stay part of Great Britain the effort to establish a free and independent Scotland continues as do efforts in many other nation states. It is perhaps worth noting that since WWII there has not been a single instance of nations combining; the European Union, being a lose confederation, an exception perhaps but with its own issue with Brexit and other nations considering their own exit. On the other hand we have seen a number of new nation states arise since WWI and WWII.

Chapter Three: Case Studies: Scotland and its relationship with Great Britain, Catalonia and Spain, Quebec and Canada

In 2024 the people of Scotland voted in a referendum regarding whether to stay a part of Great Britain or to become independent. The vote was to remain in Great Britain. A large issue was whether under Brexit Scotland wanted to remain a part of the European Union while the rest of Great Britain had voted to leave. A parting which was accomplished late in 2020.

With the results in from all 32 council areas, the "No" side won with 2,001,926 votes over 1,617,989 for "Yes". Or 55% in favor of remaining in Great Britain and 45% voting to leave. However, with the separation of Great Britain from the European Union the support for Scottish independence has gained momentum and, as in the United States and elsewhere in the world, Covid and the response to it has become a potent political force.
https://www.npr.org/2020/12/15/946242592/

support-for-scottish-independence-is-growing-partly-due-to-u-k-s-covid-19-respon

And as the NPR report makes clear a recent poll showed 58% of Scots were in favor of independence. Of course, in recent years we are all aware that polls are lacking in accuracy both because the pollsters may have tilted questions the way they wanted or because with advance of technology it is more difficult to obtain accurate samples or with political divides some may avoid polling completely thereby rendering the polls useless as tools of prediction and more political tools to advance a given agenda. But if this poll is accurate then another referendum may well be forthcoming.

Of course, this raises the question of the rights of Scotland to secede from Great Britain. A subject discussed in this article. https://www.centreonconstitutionalchange.ac.uk/news-and-opinion/does-scotland-have-right-secede One part of the discussion is who can vote on the matter. There are significant number of Englanders who reside in Scotland for example and a number of Scots who reside outside the country. And they raise an interesting point. And that is whether the vote is restricted to Scotland or whether all of the British nation should vote on the separation.

"Perhaps a better argument for restricting the vote to Scottish residents is that Scotland is a nation and as a nation it has a right to self-determination. Here we encounter the principle of national self-determination over which so much ink, and blood, has already been spilled. I have nothing to say regarding the principle apart from to note one of its obvious drawbacks: its inability to resolve matters when more than one nation claims a portion of territory. Many people, inside and outside of Scotland, believe that there is such a thing as a British nation, not just a British state. Assuming that they are right, does the British nation not have just as much of a right to national self-determination as Scotland? If so, shouldn't everyone who belongs to the British nation get a vote, not just those in Scotland?"

Of course, allowing for a national vote on the issue would very likely result in denial of the right of self-determination by the Scottish people. And this argument is likely to continue for some time as the issue ebbs and flows.

And the example of Spain denying the right of regions of the country from seceding from Spain is cited as going against actual separation of Scotland even if a significant number of Scots wish such separation. Catalonia has voted to separate from Spain, but Spain has failed to recognize its right to self-determination and separation. https://www.eyes-on-europe.eu/catalonia-the-right-to-self-determination-and-the-rule-of-law/ and among the arguments made are these which are equally applicable to the United States.

"Self-determination of peoples is a fundamental principle of contemporary international law, by virtue of which all peoples have the right to decide independently of their own political, economic and social order. Although this principle has become part of the core of norms which are indispensable to the protection of fundamental values of the international community, it continues to be characterized by margins of legal uncertainty, both in terms of the subjective scope of application, particularly with respect to the identification of target groups of the corresponding right; both regard the possibility that this right may be exercised outside the colonial context in order to lead to the creation of a new state."

It remains a thorny issue to the extent to which a minority population can exercise its rights of self-determination in order to create a new governmental entity. In this regard the article above makes the following observations:

"International law does not recognize the hypothesis that the application of the right to self-determination could be possible for a national minority because it is not considered like the population of a State, but there is a hypothesis which is worth analyzing in relation to the current situation in Catalonia. It is the one in which a State itself recognizes the right to self-determination of several « constituent » peoples; in these cases, as the Badinter Commission points out in its Opinion no. 2 on the right to self-determination of Serbs populations in Croatia and Bosnia-Herzegovina, the constituent people have the right to exercise their own self-determination within the established boundaries; consequently, the revocation of fundamental prerogatives recognized by the domestic law of the State in favor of a constituent people may constitute a violation to the right of self-determination."

As in the case of the Serbs and Croatia the issues of ethnic identity (and hatred) were certainly a factor in favor of the separation. Do significant political and constitutional differences likewise justify separation of a new governmental entity when the population of a given province or state so desires?

In the case of Spain their constitution contains a provision that would indicate that separation may require a different standard. Again, citing from the article above: "Article 2 of the Spanish Constitution reads: "The Constitution is based on the indissoluble unity of the Spanish nation, the common and indivisible country of all Spaniards; it recognizes and guarantees the right to autonomy of the nationalities and regions of which it is composed, and the solidarity amongst them all".

And further, "Article 2 is the focal point of all the Catalan situation, a nation of indissoluble unity that recognizes being composed of a plurality of nationalities. A nation that cannot recognize and accept constitutionally a pro-independence referendum. Based on Article 2, the Spanish Constitutional Court ruled that the Catalan referendum was absolutely unconstitutional. This article, however, which speaks of « plurality of nationalities », opens up the debate on the right of self-determination of the « constituent peoples » that the Badinter Commission has defined for the peoples of the former Yugoslavia and for Croatia and Bosnia and Herzegovina."

This also raises the issue of whether a people having agreed at one time to a national unity can later decide to dissolve that unity in favor of the rights of self-determination. An argument that is not likely resolved in the near future.

The final case study to consider is Quebec which has from time to time wanted to consider separation from Canada. Despite the dual language of French and English in Canada Quebec is uniquely French in character and like the Basques or Catalonians in Spain considers itself a unique and distinct province in Canada. As this article from 2018 notes Brexit has stirred many sub national groups who are flexing their muscles in an attempt to create new nation states. https://www.globalpolicyjournal.com/blog/07/06/2018/self-determination-quebec-will-old-sparks-reignite-eyes-world-fall-charlevoix

As the article notes the Supreme Court of Canada has considered and rejected the right of Quebec to secede from Canada under both the Canadian constitution and international law. https://www.canlii.org/en/ca/scc/doc/1998/1998canlii793/1998canlii793.html But of course that is hardly determinative as ultimately this is a matter of political will as much as legality.

   As with other areas such as Scotland and Catalonia (as well as the Basque region of Spain) the issue of separation continues to arise waiting perhaps for an event or a collection of grievances that will result in a rallying of public opinion in favor of secession. It would take a major event in all likelihood for this to result in more than a nascent movement into separation. Or perhaps that straw on the camel's back. But the possibility certainly continues to exist in all of these sub national constituencies.

   On the assumption that a state or province or even a section of a national entity may withdraw from a union to form its own political entity there are practical considerations what have to be taken into account and the next chapter deals with such issues.

Chapter Four: Practical Considerations of Secession and Creation of a New Union

An early discussion of problems in separation of culturally diverse populations that have formed a nation state can be found in the following article: Connor, Walker. "Self-Determination: The New Phase." *World Politics*, vol. 20, no. 1, 1967, pp. 30–53. *JSTOR*, www.jstor.org/stable/2009726. And a symposium on the issue may be useful to consider. https://www.usip.org/sites/default/files/pwks7.pdf which discusses possible policy considerations for the United States in considering the self-determination issues that arise in foreign countries.

One of the more extensive and thoughtful discussions of self-determination and rights of secession are set for the in the Oxford Max Planck Encyclopedia of International Law in 2009 which discusses a number of recent attempts both successful and unsuccessful for secession from a union. The legal aspects of such separation as well as examples to consider. Included is a discussion of Quebec which has for some time sought to separate itself from Canada. So far unsuccessfully.

https://opil.ouplaw.com/view/10.1093/law:epil/9780199231690/law-9780199231690-e1100

Assuming for the sake of argument that the legal preconditions for a state to secede from a national union exist and that a new state is created there are formidable issues to be confronted. These include:

Creation of borders of the new state and its ongoing relations with its former union partners. In light of the acrimony that likely will accompany a separation difficulty of ongoing relations may be difficult. For example: what of the military operations of the respective states. To what extent is the new state entitled to take over military facilities and equipment? What of indebtedness of the old union. To what extent is the new state responsible for debts or portions of debts of the old union. Failure to arrange for such financial considerations could result in substantial disruption to the economies of both the old union and the newly formed state. Currency of course will be an immediate issue as will other economic considerations. One argument for not allowing secession is stability and there is no question that separation of states based on controversies will result in instability. But the question is whether that instability is worse than the instability created by allowing a union of disagreeing populations to continue. We saw the problems in Serbia and Croatia where ethnic and cultural differences resulted in war and disruption on a major scale. No one who watched the Sarajevo Olympics in 1984 could not be affected by the heart-rending scenes of violence that erupted there until the two were separated into separate nation states. Is that the price of stability?

The difficulties of Great Britain in separating from the European Union while not of the same nature as separation of states as occurred in the former Yugoslavia or Czechoslovakia the pains of Brexit and difficulties that continue to this day are significant. And such issues should cause any who consider a self-determination movement to pause and consider the outcome. Not that it should prevent a secession where the circumstances justify a new nation state, but it should be a last step in a long discussion of the consequences.

Perhaps it is useful to consider the dissolution of Czechoslovakia in 1993.

https://www.newworldencyclopedia.org/entry/Dissolution_of_Czechoslovakia

This dissolution has been perhaps one of the more successful exercises in self-determination as it resulted in two separate states, which have maintained essentially cordial relations. Not that the separation was easy or uneventful. This entry in the New World Encyclopedia is well worth reading as to how the agreement was reach for separation and how property was allocated including military assets, but some issues remained unresolved for years such as the gold reserves. Initially the same currency was used but with both countries joining the EU the EU currency was later substituted. Questions of dual citizenship not allowed at the start was later permitted. Many of the issues resolved in this dissolution could be valuable for other nations facing secession issues and seeking to resolve their differences as amicably as possible.

The issues which would have to be resolved in event of separation of areas such as Scotland, Catalonia and Quebec among others would be thorny in the extreme. How to handle the social safety net, overall debt of the new and old state, military operations and so many other factors that those proposing separation would need to seriously consider. And the risks of armed conflict is a serious matter as well. For example, were Taiwan or Hong Kong or Macao to try and exercise self-determination and separate completely from mainland China one can only imagine the reaction of the CPC to such a move. Their level of tolerance is not a high bar to military action.

Self-determination as a concept developed mainly after WWI but it was rooted in history from days of the American revolution if not before. After WWII it became a strong support for de- colonization and has its modern roots in the separation of former colonies from its European nation states. But the concept continues to be debated as it applies to subnational groups desiring a national identity. In a world of globalization, it is not surprising that these aspirations are contrary to the international corporate business empires as well as political ruling classes of existing nation states. But those groups such as Scotland, Catalonia and Quebec who desire new nation state have to consider all the consequences of such an action before taking the step in to the abyss that can be the result of forming a new nation state. The complexity cannot be overstated.

Chapter Five: In Conclusion

It is not the purpose of this short book to take a position with regard to self-determination as it affects existing nation states with populations in sufficient discord to seek dissolution similar to that of Yugoslavia or Czechoslovakia but to introduce the reader to the legal, political and economic aspects of a concept proving to be as complex as self-determination.

There can be no doubt that should a significant part of a current nation state wishes to form a new union of a sub national group that opposition to such a dissolution will be swift and politically intense. Nor would such a separation probably be as amicable as that in Czechoslovakia. But hopefully it would also not be as destructive as in the case of Yugoslavia. Can there be little doubt that a separation would be preferable to a civil war with consequences for all parties as damaging as in the case of Yugoslavia or in the first civil war in the

United States? No one in their right mind would want to see that consequence. So as difficult as it might be to contemplate a separation into two or more states it is a matter that is likely to be considered and debated with much heat and disagreement whenever a sub national group is strong enough to insist on its self-determination.

    Should such separation occur it is possible that a new confederation of the divided states would allow for some continued cooperation and united effort similar to the British commonwealth or the European Union or in Czechoslovakia. One can only hope that when the issue arises that cooler heads will prevail and what is best for the peoples of nation state affected will be the determining factor in any outcome.

January 2021

www.ingramcontent.com/pod-product-compliance
Lightning Source LLC
Chambersburg PA
CBHW050323220526
45465CB00005B/2106